Capitalism and Racial Oppression

Restoring the African Mind Research Collection

The Roots of Capitalism in Europe

The origins of capitalism can be traced back to the late Middle Ages in Europe. The decline of feudalism and the rise of towns and cities created a new class of merchants and traders. These individuals began accumulating wealth through commerce which led to the emergence of a market economy. This period, often referred to as "proto-capitalism," was marked by the gradual shift from a subsistence economy to one based on trade and the exchange of goods.

One of the key developments during this period was the rise of mercantilism in the 16th and 17th centuries. Mercantilism was a system in which the state played a central role in regulating the economy to increase national wealth. It emphasized the accumulation of gold and silver, the establishment of colonies, and the protection of domestic industries through tariffs. While mercantilism was not capitalism in its purest form, it laid the groundwork for the development of capitalist economies by promoting trade and the accumulation of capital.

The Industrial Revolution, which began in the late 18th century in Britain, marked a turning point in the history of capitalism. The invention of new technologies, such as the steam engine and mechanized looms, transformed production processes and led to the growth of factories. This shift from artisanal production to mass production not only increased efficiency but also required significant capital investment. As a result, the role of capitalists—those who owned and controlled the means of production—became more prominent.

Karl Marx, who emerged as one of the most prominent critics of capitalism, developed a historical theory of class struggle based on studying the historical development of Western Europe. He pointed out that Europe started with communalism. This was a stage in which property was collectively owned. This was followed by slavery in which slaves worked for their masters. This was then followed by feudalism. Unlike slaves, the feudal serfs were not the property of the master. The serf worked on land which belonged to a manor or estate. When the manor changed hands, the serfs remained and continued to work for the landlord. Finally, came capitalism in which machines generated the greatest wealth in society. Capitalism was also marked by greater freedom and social mobility for the laborers. Whereas slaves belonged to slave owners and serfs belonged to estates, workers in the capitalist system are free to pursue work for whomever will hire them. Of course, this freedom to seek work is still restricted by the fact that the bourgeoisie in the capitalist system retains ultimate control over a worker's destiny, but the worker in capitalism has more freedom than the slave and the serf had.

Yet another feature of capitalism is greater division of labor. Division of labor refers to the separation of tasks within the economic system. For example, a teacher performs the task of educating students. Teachers are individuals who specialize in providing education. This is a different task than a musician who specializes in making music and who serves the function of providing entertainment. This is also different from the factory worker who is trained to perform the task of working in a factory to produce goods. The task of the factory worker is different from the farmer who is trained in producing food.

Division of labor ensures the effective management of a given economy by ensuring that individuals are paid to perform the tasks which they are skilled at performing. These different tasks are necessary to sustain the economic system as a whole. For example, farmers produce food so that the factory worker does not need to worry about growing his own food. This creates specialization, which means that an individual professional can specialize as a worker in his or her field without having to worry about managing other aspects of the society.

The author Bryan Ward-Perkins explained that civilizations are very complex and that everyone relies on the comfort which this complexity gives us. He gave the example of sitting in a room with good heating and an internet connection. He noted that these things were basic to his existence and yet it takes a very complex social organization to sustain this. He also noted that hundreds of thousands of people are involved in sustaining this complex social organization. This network of specialization is what makes it possible for Ward-Perkins to sit in a heated room with an internet connection. I mention this to make the point that capitalism was more than a mere shift in production. The emergence of capitalism resulted in a complex form of social organization which can only be sustained by specialization and division of labor.

Under feudalism, peasants were bound to the land. This provided little incentive to increase output beyond subsistence because most of their labor's surplus was claimed by the lord. This lack of motivation meant agricultural productivity grew slowly. One advantage which capitalism maintained over feudalism was that in capitalism individuals have the ability to acquire a greater share of the surplus for their labor. Workers have strong incentives to maximize efficiency because their rewards are tied directly to their output. This drive for higher productivity has allowed capitalist economies to sustain larger populations and improve standards of living in ways feudal economies could not.

In addition to providing a greater opportunity to acquire wealth through increased productivity, capitalism has also tended to encourage innovations. Technological progress was slow during the feudal era. Capitalism, by contrast, encourages competition. In order to gain an advantage, capitalists are constantly seeking better methods, tools, and technologies. This dynamic has led to revolutionary developments such as the Industrial Revolution, which transformed economies and drastically increased global wealth. This drive towards innovation to gain an edge over competition is another aspect of capitalism which allowed it to surpass the previous modes of production in terms of productivity and efficiency.

Marx himself argued that capitalism was a very productive system. He stated: "The bourgeoisie, during its rule of scarce one hundred years, has created more massive and more colossal productive forces than have all preceding generations together. Subjection of Nature's forces to man, machinery, application of chemistry to industry and agriculture, steam-navigation, railways, electric telegraphs, clearing of whole continents for cultivation, canalization of rivers, whole populations conjured out of the ground—what earlier century had even a presentiment that such productive forces slumbered in the lap of social labor?"

In Marx's view, capitalism was to follow the same fate as

slavery and feudalism. Though capitalism provided greater freedoms for the laborer and provided technological advancements which improved quality of life, Marx believed that capitalism would eventually fall and that a new system would emerge. Marx envisioned that the working class would rise up and overthrow the capitalist ruling class to produce a new society. This new society would be a communist society in which the workers themselves had control over the means of production.

As it would turn out, Marx's theory was not completely accurate. In his book *To Have or To Be?* Erich Fromm argued that the problem with Marx was that he lived a hundred years too soon. Fromm explained that Marx and Engels both believed that capitalism had reached the end of its possibilities and that the revolution would soon come. Engels later admitted after Marx's death that this was a mistaken view.

Marx's predictions about the fall of capitalism may not have bene accurate, but Marx did lay the historical background to the development of capitalism as a particular stage in the history of Europe's economic development. As Marx noted, this was a stage which was marked by increased productivity. The rise of capitalism also coincided with the rise of European imperialism and the rise of European racism.

The Development of Racism

Humans have always recognized differences in physical traits and cultural traits, but race is a concept which emerged within Western civilization during the age of colonialism to justify the Western colonization of people who were not deemed to be white. White itself represented the physical appearances of Europeans who recognized that the complexions of others around the world were much darker than their own. Out of this concept of race came racism, which was built on the notion white people were a superior race and that people should be defined by their racial identity. Out of racism emerged systems such as Jim Crow and apartheid, which upheld white supremacy at the expense of black people who were deemed to be inferior.

It is important to note here that racism may have been one of Western civilization's negative aspects, but racism in Western civilization was not a feature which was present in its early Greco-Roman roots. Frank Snowden demonstrated that in ancient Greco-Roman society, there was no prejudice associated with skin color. Snowden explained that "both Greeks and Romans, notwithstanding a few concepts and ideas sometimes misinterpreted as anti-black in sentiment, had the ability to see and to comment on the obviously different physical characteristics of Ethiopians without developing an elaborate and rigid system of discrimination based on the color of the skin." Color prejudice in Europe did become more noticeable. In one of his lectures, Eusi Kwayana noted that in William Shakespeare's play, *The Merchant of Venice*, a man from Morocco seeks to marry a woman named Portia. Much of their interaction was centers on the complexion of the Moroccan man, who asks Portia to mislike him not because of his dark complexion. The Moroccan man fails in his attempt to marry Portia because he selects the wrong casket. This causes Portia to remark, "Let all of his complexion choose me so." Kwayana mentioned this to show that prejudice based on skin color did exist in Europe before racism became institutionalized.

James Sweet argued that racial prejudice was introduced to Europe by the Moors when the Moors had conquered Iberia. As Sweet noted, Arabs developed their own racist views against

African people. Sweet argued that "many Iberian Christians had internalized the racist attitudes of the Muslims and were applying them to the increasing flow of African slaves to their part of the world." This seems plausible, but my focus here is not so much on where racism in Western civilization emerged from. My point is that racism was not a feature of Western civilization in the early development of Western civilization. Racism became more prominent in the 1500s and onward.

In his book *Capitalism and Slavery*, Eric Williams explained: "Slavery was not born of racism: rather, racism was the consequence of slavery." In *How Europe Underdeveloped Africa*, Walter Rodney, utilizing a Marxist analysis of history, traced the roots of racism in Europe to slavery and the emergence of capitalism. He noted that the enslavement of African people was not done for racist reasons, but rather that racism developed as a means to rationalize the enslavement of African people. As the capitalist system developed, Rodney noted that racism became an integral part of the capitalist mode of production. Rodney was also careful to point out that it would be too sweeping a statement to suggest that all racial prejudice in Europe derived from the enslavement of Africans and the exploitation of other non-white groups. The example he gave was anti-Semitism in Europe, which predated capitalism. This would suggest that racial prejudice in Europe became part of the mode of production due to colonialism and the emergence of capitalism, but that within Western society there was already a tendency towards extreme prejudice towards other groups.

The idea of race itself is not so much the problem. Physical differences exist. The problem with white supremacy is that white supremacists believe that differences suggest that there must be inferior and superior races. On his hajj to Mecca, Malcolm X shared the profound experience of worshiping alongside white people. Malcolm had believed Elijah Muhammad's teachings that white people were devils by nature, but his experience in Mecca brought him in contact with people who were physically white, but to them being white represented incidental characteristics. Malcolm contrasted this with white identity in American society, in which white means "boss." White within a white supremacist society is not merely an incidental physical trait, but a social status which represents power and domination.

Within a capitalist framework, the concept of race became tied to labor relations. This is why Williams noted that racism was born out of slavery. The plantations of the New World are where race became institutionalized and became tied to wealth. This is not to suggest that forms of racial prejudice did not exist, but there was no institutionalized system of racism in Western society prior to the European colonization of the New World.

The system of white supremacy which Europeans constructed was one which varied from colonial society to colonial society. In the United States, for example, the one-drop rule developed as a means to classify anyone with a drop of African blood as being an African in the United States. This was not the case in countries such as Brazil or South Africa where mixed race individuals were treated differently than those who were black. The conception of white identity differed as well. For example, the Portuguese in Guyana were not regarded as being white because they came to Guyana as indentured laborers. White as an identity developed as one which was related to power. In colonial Guyana, the Portuguese did not have power as the British did, so they were not viewed as being white within that context. The Portuguese faced discrimination as well in Guyana because they did not fit into the construct of being white in Guyana.

Even with these variations, what was clear was within this system of plantation Africans were not only regarded as inferior, but the very racial identity of Africans was tied to being slave labor. This was not only an aspect of the social life in the New World, but it became encoded in law. In *Hudgins v. Wright*, 1 Hen. & M. 134 (1806), the Wrights were able to successfully obtain their freedom. The reasoning which Judge Tucker of the Supreme Court of Appeals of Virginia provided for ruling that the Wrights were to be freed demonstrated the racial attitudes surrounding slavery at the time. The Wrights appeared white and were descendants of a free Native American woman. Judge Tucker explained that if a black or mulatto woman were to appear before a judge on the writ of habeas corpus, on the ground of false imprisonment and detention in slavery, the judge "must redeliver the black or mulatto person, with the flat nose and woolly hair to the person claiming to hold him or her as a slave, unless the black person or mulatto could procure some person to be bound for him, to produce proof of his descent, in the maternal line, from a *free female ancestor*." Judge Tucker also explained that the first clause of the Bill of Rights "was meant to embrace the case of free citizens, or aliens only; and not by a side wind to overturn the rights of property, and give freedom to those very people whom we have been compelled from imperious circumstances to retain, generally, in the same state of bondage that they were in at the revolution, in which they had no *concern, agency* or *interest*."

In *Dred Scott v. Sandford*, 60 U.S. (19 How.) 393 (1857), the Supreme Court held that African people did not have any rights which a white man was bound to respect. Chief Justice Roger Taney, who delivered the opinion of the Supreme Court, explained that Africans "had for more than a century before been regarded as beings of an inferior order, and altogether unfit to associate with the white race either in social or political relations, and so far inferior that they had no rights which the white man was bound to respect, and that the negro might justly and lawfully be reduced to slavery for his benefit. He was bought and sold, and treated as an ordinary article of merchandise and traffic whenever a profit could be made by it." Based on this reasoning, the Supreme Court held that Dred Scott did not have standing to bring a suit in federal court. These two rulings make it clear that in the United States, race was tied to having rights under the law.

In *Psychopathic Racial Personality and Other Essays*, Bobby E. Wright argued that African Americans "are the world's only legally created group, (created through the 13th, 14th, and 15th amendments which can be repealed at any moment by the Congress or declared unconstitutional by the Supreme Court)." Wright's statement spoke to the very precarious legal situation which African Americans have been in. Congress has never repealed these amendments, but historically Congress has not consistently enforced the protections offered by these amendments. The Supreme Court has never declared the amendments unconstitutional, but the Supreme Court has certainly limited the protections offered by these amendments and has also limited the protections offered by civil rights legislation. In other words, Congress and the Supreme Court have not eliminated the legislation which was implemented to provide African Americans with the rights of citizenship, but such rights have been abridged so as to also protect the right of white people to discriminate as they see fit.

The Fourteenth Amendment was the amendment which provided citizenship for African Americans. The amendment reads:

> All persons born or naturalized in the United States, and subject to the jurisdiction thereof, are citizens of the United States and of the State wherein they reside. No State shall make or enforce any law which shall abridge the privileges or immunities of citizens of the United States; nor shall any State deprive any person of life, liberty, or property, without due process of law; nor deny to any person within its jurisdiction the equal protection of the laws.

The Fourteenth Amendment, in theory, provided equal status for African Americans. In practice, however, African Americans continued to endure racism and the deprivation of the rights which white citizens enjoyed. This has even included white immigrant groups who arrived in the United States after African Americans did. Although some European immigrant groups such as Italians and Irish did endure discrimination and prejudice in America, African Americans have been the group that has been consistently denied of their constitutional rights, to such an extent that it has required several amendments to the Constitution and the passage of civil right laws to protect the constitutional rights of African Americans; rights which are due to American citizens at birth.

Consider the fact that the Constitution itself had to be altered to provide more protections to African Americans. The Constitution had to be amended just so that persons of African descent who were born free in the United States could be regarded as being equal with white citizens. Consider the numerous civil rights bills that were passed for the purpose of providing equal treatment and equal protection to African Americans. This is what Bobby E.

Wright referred to when he stated that African Americans were a legally created people. It took the alteration of American law for African Americans to be regarded as equals under that very law. This created a separate legal status for African Americans, which was much different from the legal status of white citizens.

The struggle to obtain equal citizenship rights must also be understood in economic terms as well because the exploitation of African Americans was not merely a form of racial oppression, but a form of economic oppression as well; a type of oppression which benefited the financial interests of white citizens. African people were dragged to the United States for the purpose of being enslaved. African people did not willingly go to America to be worked as slaves. Moreover, slavery was an industry which many individuals profited from. Slaves were a commodity, which were bought and sold on auction blocks. The slave also worked for the slave master without pay.

The primary reason why Africans were brought to the United States was to be utilized for slave labor. For this reason, when the United States was founded, the laws which were implemented were laws which were consistent with America's slave society. The laws were also consistent with the white supremacist views held by some of the Founding Fathers. Thomas Jefferson, for example, expressed the view that "the blacks, whether originally a distinct race, or made distinct by time and circumstances, are inferior to the whites in the endowments both of body and mind."

The United States was not formed with the interests and the well-being of African people being a central focus. This was so painfully true that despite the horrible conditions which enslaved Africans had to endure inside of the slave ships which brought them to America, the Constitution ensured that the slave trade would be protected until 1801. Article 1, Section 9, Clause 1 reads: "The Migration or Importation of such Persons as any of the States now existing shall think proper to admit, shall not be prohibited by the Congress prior to the Year one thousand eight hundred and eight, but a Tax or duty may be imposed on such Importation, not exceeding ten dollars for each Person."

Newly liberated Africans were now making the transition away from being commodities in a slave society to being laborers in a capitalistic society. Slavery itself had played a significant role in the development of Western capitalism. This is a point that Eric Williams documented in his book *Capitalism and Slavery*. Unlike slaves, the worker in a capitalistic system is not owned by a master. In the system of capitalism, a worker freely contracts to provide his or her laborer to an employer who pays the worker a wage in return for the worker's labor. Whereas a slave is made to work against his or her will—often through the threat of force—the worker is compelled to work because the worker needs to earn a wage in order to pay for necessities such as food and shelter.

In the relationship between the employer and the employee, the employer generally maintains the dominant position. One does not have to adhere to Karl Marx's theories to understand that within the system of capitalism contradictions between the worker and the employer can and do arise. Marx envisioned that the working class would one day rebel against the capitalist ruling class and that this revolution would bring forward a communist society in which the means of production are commonly owned by the workers themselves rather than being owned and controlled by a few capitalists who profit from the labor of the working class.

America was never subjected to the type of communist inspired revolution which Russia experienced, but America certainly has not been immune to struggles between the working class and the owners of the means of production. The dangers of unrestrained capitalism are precisely why Marx envisioned an eventual uprising on the part of the working class, which would overturn the exploitative capitalist system. Such a revolution may very well have been inevitable in industrialized capitalist countries if not for reforms and regulations which restrict the power of the employer and provide protections for the employee. Far from overturning a system in which the working class labors for wages, the reforms ensure that the working class is not overworked and underpaid. These regulations have also ensured that children cannot be employed to work as laborers and that workers can be compensated if they are injured while working.

African people found themselves oppressed not only within a society that implemented a very strict racial hierarchy, but also a system with a class hierarchy as well. It is for this reason that civil rights legislation can be understood to be not only about protecting African Americans from racial discrimination, but also about protecting working people from being exploited by their employers. After all, an African who was denied a job on account of his or her race was not only being discriminated against racially but was also a victim of a capitalist system which places the worker at the mercy of the employer. Again, one does not need to adhere to the theories of Marx to understand that in an economic system where one's survival is based on the ability to earn a wage from an employer, there is an inherent inequality that can be easily exploited to the benefit of the employer and to the detriment of the employee.

The Supreme Court has often struggled with maintaining the balance between allowing capitalists to freely engage in the pursuit of enriching themselves and regulating businesses for the purpose of protecting the interests of workers. Where the two interests clashed, there were times when the Supreme Court took the side of the capitalist employer over that of the worker. This was very apparent during the so-called Lochner Era. This era is so called because of *Lochner v. New York*, 198 U.S. 45 (1905), which was a case in which the Supreme Court struck down a New York state law that regulated the working hours of bakers. *Lochner* was one of several cases in which the Supreme Court struck down measures that were implemented to improve the conditions of American workers.

In *Lochner*, Justice Rufus Peckham, who delivered the opinion, declared that the "general right to make a contract in relation to his business is part of the liberty of the individual protected by the Fourteenth Amendment of the Federal Constitution." Justice Peckham continued to explain that the "right to purchase or to sell labor is part of the liberty protected by this amendment, unless there are circumstances which exclude the right." The Supreme Court in *Lochner* held that working hours for bakers was not one of those circumstances where the right to purchase and sell labor should be abridged. Justice Peckham explained: "There is no reasonable ground for interfering with the liberty of person or the right of free contract, by determining the hours of labor, in the occupation of a baker."

Justice Peckham cited *Holden v. Hardy*, 169 U.S. 366 (1989) which was a case in which the Supreme Court held that a law limiting the work hours of miners and smelters was a valid exercise of police power by the State, but Justice Peckham explained that the ruling in *Holden* did not apply in *Lochner*. Peckham explained that the law limiting the work hours of bakers was not related to protecting the safety of the bakers or the well-being of the public, as clean and wholesome "bread does not depend upon whether the baker works but ten hours per day or only sixty hours a week."

Peckham indicated that limiting the work hours of bakers was not as serious a concern as limiting the working hours of miners, but there was yet another issue that factored into the Supreme Court's ruling in *Lochner*. That issue was the power of the State versus the liberty of individuals. Justice Peckham explained as much when he framed the case as being "a question of which of two powers or rights shall prevail—the power of the State to legislate or the right of the individual to liberty of person and freedom of contract." In this case, the right of individual liberty and freedom of contract prevailed.

In *Lochner*, Peckham declared that "the liberty of contract relating to labor includes both parties to it. The one has as much right to purchase as the other to sell labor." The rights are not equal, however. In a capitalist economy, the party contracting for the purchase of labor typically has a number of advantages over the party contracting to sell his or her labor. A most obvious advantage is that the employee relies on the income he or she receives from the employer. For this reason, the employer is in a better position to dictate the terms of employment to the employee.

Yet another advantage which employers enjoy is the at-will doctrine, which allows an employer to discharge an employee for any reason at all. The Supreme Court of Alabama in *Allied Supply Co. v. Brown*, 585 So. 2d 33, 35 (Ala.1991) described the doctrine as thus: "Employees at will can terminate their employment, or can be terminated by their employer, at any time, with or without cause or justification." The Supreme Court of Alabama noted that the "at-will" doctrine has been criticized as being harsh, but that it remained the law in Alabama. The Supreme Court of Tennessee held in *Payne v. Western & Atlantic. R.R.*, 81 Tenn. (1884) that men "must be left, without interference to buy and sell where they please, and to discharge or retain employees at will for good cause or for no cause, or even for bad cause without thereby being guilty of an unlawful act per se."

The Supreme Court of Tennessee in *Payne* quoted Judge Cooley, who stated: "It is a part of every man's civil rights that he be at liberty to refuse business relations with any person whomsoever, whether the refusal rests upon reason, or is the result of whim, caprice, prejudice or malice. With his reasons neither the public nor third persons have any legal concern." The logic expressed by Cooley here is precisely the type of logic used to defend racial segregation. Under such reasoning, it would be the civil right of every man to deny business relations to an African American solely on the basis of prejudice and it would not be of any legal concern to the African American who is denied business relations.

Should racists be forced to contract with African Americans? Holding such a view necessarily entails that certain rights on the part of the racist individual will be curtailed or infringed upon. How far then can the law go to establish racial equality? How far should the law go? These are questions that must be asked in order to assess the role that legislation has played in attempting to resolve the problem of racial discrimination in the United States. Prior to the civil rights movement, courts adopted the view that the law must not go too far in imposing against the segregationist because doing so would infringe on one's freedom to reject engaging in business relations with whomever one pleases and for whatever reason one chooses.

There is also the question of whether or not it is practical for racial problems to be addressed through imposing racial integration against the will of the racists. The argument against this is not only that it infringes upon the rights of the racist, but that it would perhaps be better for African Americans to avoid being around racists who harbor such negative, bigoted, and hateful views. Perhaps it may be in the best interests of African Americans to avoid such racist individuals altogether. The problem with this approach is that racial separation in of itself is not a solution to the problem so long as rules which are designed to restrict the rights of African Americans remain in place.

As a minister of the Nation of Islam, Malcolm X drew a distinction between segregation and racial separation. In an interview with Eleanor Fischer, Malcolm X explained his views, stating: "Segregation is that which is forced upon an inferior by a superior. Separation is done voluntarily by two equals." Segregation was imposed upon African Americans. Segregation was the law and this law was implemented to enforce racial inequality.

What of separation? Malcolm X said that separation was done on a voluntary basis by two equals. The problem here is that there was an unequal relationship and for this reason African Americans were not free to build separately or independently from the dominant white society. The Nation of Islam preached a doctrine of racial separation. To achieve this vision of separation, Elijah Muhammad advocated the creation of a separate state for black people. The Nation of Islam was free to preach separation, but the Nation of Islam lacked the power or capacity to truly carry out this separation and the American government was certainly not going to give into the Nation of Islam's demands for land to build a separate nation. The Republic of New Afrika also demanded land to create a separate black nation.

Just as those who struggled for integration were met with a backlash, the Nation of Islam and other black separatist organizations were met with a similar backlash. Segregation was the law. Any attempts at racial integration were therefore a violation of that law, yet the segregationists did not view the black separatists as being preferable to the integrationists. On the contrary, black nationalism and the doctrine of black separation was viewed as a threat because it was an assertion of African American independence. The entire purpose of segregation was to keep African Americans in their place; to keep African Americans oppressed and subjugated. Integration was a threat to the status quo, but assertions of African American independence were also a threat as well because it was contrary to the goal of keeping African Americans subjugated.

Due to the threat of African American independence, building separate institutions from white people has been a challenge because when African Americans have done so it has been perceived as competing against white interests and eliminated for this reason. Ida B. Wells-Barnett was a well-known anti-lynching activist whose activism was motivated by the fact that her friend Thomas Moss had been lynched because Moss opened a grocery store, which was seen as a threat to a nearby white owned grocery store. African Americans did not have the freedom to patronize white owned businesses, but African Americans could not open and operate their own businesses without facing discrimination either. Therefore, separation alone is not a solution so long as African people do not have the necessary protection from white aggression.

Now that the matter of racial segregation has been briefly addressed, we shall return again to the manner in which the Supreme Court ruled on labor issues during the Lochner Era. In 1919, the Congress passed the Child Labor Law tax which imposed a tax on companies which employed child labor. A furniture manufacturer known as the Drexel Furniture Company incurred a ten percent tax on its net profits for allowing a fourteen year old boy to work in its factories. In *Bailey v. Drexel Furniture Co.*, 259 U.S. 20 (1922), the Supreme Court held that this tax imposed on Drexel was unconstitutional.

President William Taft, who was then serving as the Chief Justice of the Supreme Court, explained that the Child Labor Law "is attacked on the ground that it is a regulation of the employment of child labor in the states—an exclusively state function under the federal Constitution and within the reservations of the Tenth Amendment." The Tenth Amendment provides that: "The powers not delegated to the United States by the Constitution, nor prohibited by it to the States, are reserved to the States respectively, or to the people." In other words, since the Constitution did not delegate to the United States the ability to restrict child labor and because the use of child labor was not prohibited to any of the states, the argument which was made against the Child Labor Tax was that it was a violation of states' rights.

The Supreme Court in this case held that the tax was unconstitutional because the taxes were in fact a penalty against businesses which utilized child labor. Taft explained that "a court must be blind not to see that the so-called tax is imposed to stop the employment of children within the age limits prescribed. Its prohibitory and regulatory effect and purpose are palpable. All others can see and understand this. How can we properly shut our minds to it?"

In *Coppage v. Kansas*, 236 U.S. 1 (1915), the Supreme Court held that it was legal for an employer to forbid an employee from joining a union. The plaintiff, Coppage, was found to be guilty of violating a state statute. Section one of that statute provided: "That it shall be unlawful for any individual or member of any firm, or any agent, officer, or employee of any company or corporation to coerce, require, demand, or influence any person or persons to enter into any agreement, either written or verbal, not to join or become or remain a member of any labor organization or association as a condition of such person or persons securing employment or continuing in the employment of such individual, firm, or corporation."

The purpose of the law was to bar employers from preventing their employees from joining unions, which was precisely what Coppage did. Hedges was employed as a switchman by the St. Louis & San Francisco Railway Company. He was also a member of a labor organization called the Switchmen's Union of North America. Coppage was employed by the railway company as superintendent. Coppage requested Hedges to sign an agreement to withdraw from Switchmen's Union. Hedges was informed that if he did not sign it then he could not remain employed.

The Supreme Court held that the law enacted by the state of Kansas violated the "due process" clause of the Fourteenth Amendment. Justice Mahlon Pitney, who delivered the opinion, stated that "it is said by the Kansas Supreme Court (87 Kansas, p. 759) to be a matter of common knowledge that 'employees, as a rule, are not financially able to be as independent in making contracts for the sale of their labor as are employers in making contracts of purchase thereof.'" Of this inequality between employees and employers in making contracts, Justice Pitney remarked that "wherever the right of private property exists, there must and will be inequalities of fortune; and thus it naturally happens that parties negotiating about a contract are not equally unhampered by circumstances." Justice Pitney continued to explain that it is self-evident that "unless all things are held in common, some persons must have more property than others, it is from the nature of things impossible to uphold freedom of contract and the right of private property without at the same time recognizing as legitimate those inequalities of fortune that are the necessary result of the exercise of those rights."

Justice Pitney seemed to have been arguing that upholding freedom of contract and the right to private property cannot be done without also creating "inequalities of fortune", which are seen as the outcome of exercising such rights. Here one may ask whose freedom of contract and right to private property was the Supreme Court interested in protecting? If it would be a violation for a state to impose laws which bar employers from preventing employees from joining unions, would it not as equally be a violation of freedom of contract for employees to be barred from joining a union? The central issue being addressed by the Supreme Court was whether or not the freedom of contract of the employer should supersede that of the employee.

In the end, the Supreme Court held that it was not a significant infringement upon the right to freedom of contract of employees to allow employers to deny employees the ability to join a union. Justice Pitney explained that to "ask a man to agree, in advance, to refrain from affiliation with the union while retaining a certain position of employment, is not to ask him to give up any part of his constitutional freedom. He is free to decline the employment on those terms, just as the employer may decline to offer employment on any other; for 'It takes two to make a bargain.'" Justice Pitney continued to note that after having accepted employment under those terms, the employee is still free to join a union after the period of his employment ends.

An employee can, as Justice Pitney noted, either decline employment on those terms, which means trying to find employment elsewhere or the employee could merely join a union after the period of employment ends. The problem with such an approach is that if an employer is free to prevent employees from joining unions then the protections offered by the ability to unionize are nullified. There also is no guarantee that an employee will even find an employer who is willing to allow employees to join unions. The Supreme Court was effectively prioritizing the freedom of an employer to deny the right to unionize to its employees over the right of an employee to join a union.

Justice Oliver Holmes wrote a dissent to the Supreme Court's ruling in *Coppage*. Justice Holmes explained: "In present conditions a workman not unnaturally may believe that only by belonging to a union can he secure a contract that shall be fair to him. [...] If that belief, whether right or wrong, may be held by a reasonable man, it seems to me that it may be enforced by law in order to establish the equality of position between the parties in which liberty of contract begins."

Holmes concluded his dissent by writing: "I therefore think that the statute of Kansas, sustained by the Supreme Court of the State, did not go beyond a legitimate exercise of the police power, when it sought, not to require one man to employ another against his will, but to put limitations upon the sacrifice of rights which one man may exact from another as a condition of employment. Entertaining these views, I am constrained to dissent from the judgment in this case."

These rulings by the Supreme Court demonstrated the conflict between a laissez-faire approach which allows businesses to do as they please and the ability of the government to regulate businesses to avoid the harsher aspects of the capitalist system. These cases also demonstrated the tensions between protecting the rights of workers, while also protecting the right to freedom of contract of the employers. As was already noted, unrestrained capitalism can be very harsh for workers, who are given very little protection from exploitation. It is for this reason that states had to enact policies to protect workers through placing regulations on employers. Relying on the good-will of the employers was simply not enough, especially when the employers had a financial incentive to exploit workers.

Federal regulations and restrictions were especially required to protect African Americans, who not only required employee protections, but racial protections as well. This is also relevant to the point mentioned previously about African Americans being a legally created people. The rights offered to American citizens in the Constitution were not rights that were readily extended to African Americans. Instead, African Americans needed separate laws merely just to be recognized as citizens and to enjoy constitutional rights, such as liberty to contact.

After the aforementioned Lochner Era, the Supreme Court began to rule in favor of regulations and restrictions. The National Labor Relations Act of 1935 was passed to allow employees the ability to unionize without interference from the employer. This legislation was ruled to be constitutional by the Supreme Court in *National Labor Relations Board v. Jones & Laughlin Steel Corporation*, 301 U.S. 1 (1937). The Supreme Court held:

That is a fundamental right. Employees have as clear a right to organize and select their representatives for lawful purposes as the respondent has to organize its business and select its own officers and agents. Discrimination and coercion to prevent the free exercise of the right of employees to self-organization and representation is a proper subject for condemnation by competent legislative authority. Long ago we stated the reason for labor organizations. We said that they were organized out of the necessities of the situation; that a single employee was helpless in dealing with an employer; that he was dependent ordinarily on his daily wage for the maintenance of himself and family; that if the employer refused to pay him the wages that he thought fair, he was nevertheless unable to leave the employ and resist arbitrary and unfair treatment; that union was essential to give laborers opportunity to deal on an equality with their employer.

In *West Coast Hotel Co. v. Parrish*, 300 U.S. 379 (1937), the Supreme Court ruled in favor of establishing a minimum wage for laborers. In this case, Elsie Parrish, who was employed as a chambermaid, brought a suit to recover the difference between the wages paid to her and the minimum wage fixed pursuant to the

Washington state law, which set minimum wage at $14.50 per week of 48 hours. Chief Justice Charles Hughes explained:

> In each case the violation alleged by those attacking minimum wage regulation for women is deprivation of freedom of contract. What is this freedom? The Constitution does not speak of freedom of contract. It speaks of liberty and prohibits the deprivation of liberty without due process of law. In prohibiting that deprivation the Constitution does not recognize an absolute and uncontrollable liberty. Liberty in each of its phases has its history and connotation.

Chief Justice Hughes also explained that the "essential limitation of liberty in general governs freedom of contract in particular." Given that the liberty to contract is not absolute, the Supreme Court does have the ability to restrict freedom of contract. In this particular case, the Supreme Court decided that freedom of contract does not prevent states from enacting regulations to protect workers. Chief Justice Hughes mentions a number of regulations which had been implemented, such as an eight-hour work day for underground miners and smelters, forbidding the payment of seamen's wages in advance, and maintaining workmen's compensation laws. Chief Justice Hughes explained that "the legislature has necessarily a wide field of discretion in order that there may be suitable protection of health and safety, and that peace and good order may be promoted through regulations designed to insure wholesome conditions of work and freedom from oppression."

The Supreme Court was also concerned with protecting workers from undue economic exploitation because when workers are denied a living wage, it is taxpayers who are made to pay the cost of living for those workers:

> There is an additional and compelling con-sideration which recent economic experience has brought into a strong light. The exploitation of a class of workers who are in an unequal position with respect to bargaining power, and are thus relatively defenceless against the denial of a living wage, is not

only detrimental to their health and wellbeing, but casts a direct burden for their support upon the community. What these workers lose in wages, the taxpayers are called upon to pay. The bare cost of living must be met.

The Supreme Court's ruling in *West Coast Hotel Co.* demonstrated that protecting workers meant limiting freedom of contract for employers. One of the fundamental principles in contract law is "freedom of contract." This refers to the freedom of persons to enter into contracts. It must be made clear that a contract is not merely an agreement between parties. A contract is a legally binding agreement and therefore the party which breaches the contract can be found to be legally liable for the breach. Contract law is based on the principle that one should be held accountable for the promises that one makes to others. Of course, not every promise is regarded by the courts as being a contract. Indeed, a contract refers to a very specific type of promise, consisting of three elements: an offer, acceptance, and consideration.

The Supreme Court held in *Dred Scott v. Sandford*, 60 U.S. (19 How.) 393 (1857) that Africans were not regarded as American citizens, regardless of if they were enslaved or freed. As such, the rights that were offered to American citizens were not enjoyed by African people. Enslaved Africans were regarded as chattel or property, which could be bought, sold, or traded. Freedom of contract meant the freedom to enter into contracts for the sale of enslaved persons. Owning an enslaved African was a property right for which the Constitution granted protection. Article IV, Section 2, Clause 3 of the Constitution reads:

No person held to service or labour in one state, under the laws thereof, escaping into another, shall, in consequence of any law or regulation therein, be discharged from such service or labor, but shall be delivered up on claim of the party to whom such service or labour may be due.

The word slave is not used in the clause, but the effect of the clause was obviously meant to ensure that slave masters had the right to have their property returned to them if that property were to escape. The right to private property protected the right of slave masters to own Africans. Much like other forms of property, banks were able to acquire a secured interest in slaves. Enslaved Africans were used as collateral for loans which were issued by banks and when borrowers defaulted on their loans, banks were able to take ownership over the slaves.

The struggles that African Americans continued to endure after the abolition of slavery was in many ways a struggle for freedom of contract. The racial segregation which followed the abolition of slavery was aimed at restricting the ability of African Americans to exercise freedom of contract. This struggle was clearly illustrated in *Civil Rights Cases*, 109 U.S. 3 (1883), which were cases that were brought before the Supreme Court regarding the first and second sections of a civil rights act which was passed by Congress on March 1, 1875, entitled "An Act to protect all citizens in their civil and legal rights."

The plaintiffs, in five cases from lower courts, were bringing suits alleging civil rights violations. The claims included denying to persons of color the accommodations and privileges of an inn and denying to individuals the privileges and accommodations of a theatre, along with other claims. In delivering the opinion of the Supreme Court, Justice Joseph Bradley explained: "The essence of the law is, not to declare broadly that all persons shall be entitled to the full and equal enjoyment of the accommodations, advantages, facilities, and privileges of inns, public conveyances, and theaters; but that such enjoyment shall not be subject to any conditions applicable only to citizens of a particular race or color, or who had been in a previous condition of servitude."

Congress' power to enact civil rights legislation rests in the Fourteenth Amendment, which stipulates that "no State shall make or enforce any law which shall abridge the privileges or immunities of citizens of the United States; nor shall any State deprive any person of life, liberty, or property without due process of law; nor deny to any person within its jurisdiction the equal protection of the laws." Justice Bradley explained that there was no question that the Fourteenth Amendment "nullifies and makes void all State legislation, and State action of every kind, which impairs the privileges and immunities of citizens of the United States, or which injures them in life, liberty, or property without due process of law, or which denies to any of them the equal protection of the laws."

Bradley explained that the Fourteenth Amendment "does not invest Congress with power to legislate upon subjects which are within the domain of State legislation; but to provide modes of relief against State legislation, or State action, of the kind referred to." Justice Bradley continued to explain that the Fourteenth Amendment "does not authorize Congress to create a code of municipal law for the regulation of private rights; but to provide modes of redress against the operation of State laws, and the action of State officers, executive or judicial, when these are subversive of the fundamental rights specified in the amendment." Bradley concluded that "until some State law has been passed, or some State action through its officers or agents has been taken, adverse to the rights of citizens sought to be protected by the Fourteenth Amendment, no legislation of the United States under said amendment, nor any proceeding under such legislation, can be called into activity: for the prohibitions of the amendment are against State laws and acts done under State authority."

In *Civil Rights Cases*, the Supreme Court, in essence, held that private citizens have the right to engage in racial segregation and that the Fourteenth Amendment does not authorize Congress to regulate the actions of private citizens who choose to discriminate on the basis of race. The problem with such an interpretation is that it severely limited the enforcement of the Fourteenth Amendment by allowing individuals to discriminate. More so than this, however, the Supreme Court ruling held that individuals could deny African Americans the freedom to contract. This will be addressed in more detail, but the point to be made here is that the Supreme Court ruling in *Civil Right Cases* undermined important pieces of legislation which were intended to ensure that African Americans were protected from discrimination, as well as given equal treatment and opportunities under the law.

Yet another problem that arises from interpreting the Fourteenth Amendment is what constitutes due process? This is important because the Fourteenth Amendment provides, as previously noted, that no "State shall make or enforce any law which shall abridge the privileges or immunities of citizens of the United States; nor shall any State deprive any person of life, liberty, or property, without due process of law; nor deny to any person within its jurisdiction the equal protection of the laws." The Fourteenth Amendment protects citizens against the arbitrary deprivation of rights and privileges, but what happens when the deprivation of such rights and privileges are written into the law and upheld by the courts? At this point the citizen is no longer being deprived of any rights without due process because the law itself enforces such deprivation of those rights.

In *Plessy v. Ferguson*, 163 U.S. 537 (1896), the Supreme Court stated, "we think the enforced separation of the races, as applied to the internal commerce of the State, neither abridges the privileges or immunities of the colored man, deprives him of his property without due process of law, nor denies him the equal protection of the laws, within the meaning of the Fourteenth Amendment [...]." The Supreme Court here was willing to permit racial segregation, stating that enforced separation of the races was not depriving an individual of the right of due process.

The laws were not so straightforward as to outright ban African Americans from voting because of their racial identity. Instead, the voting restrictions appeared to be racially neutral on their face. This included policies such as a poll tax, which required voters to pay a tax in order to register to vote. On its face a poll tax appears racially neutral. In fact, poll taxes have historically barred white citizens from voting just as it has barred black citizens, but the "grandfather clause" was one of the means by which white citizens could escape the requirement of a poll tax. The grandfather clause exempted individuals who were able to vote prior to January 1, 1867, or individuals who were the son or grandson of an individual who could vote prior to that time. Prior to 1867, African Americans were not eligible to vote in Louisiana and for this reason the grandfather clause would not apply.

In *Louisiana v. United States*, 380 U.S. 145 (1965), the Supreme Court held that Louisiana's voter restriction policies were unconstitutional. In 1921, Louisiana replaced the grandfather clause with an "interpretation test" which required an applicant for registration to "give a reasonable interpretation" of any clause in Louisiana's Constitution or the Constitution of the United States. From the adoption of the 1921 interpretation test until 1944, African Americans never exceeded one percent of the registered voting population. Prior to 1944, African Americans only had a slight interest in voting since Louisiana's laws prevented African Americans from voting in the Democratic Party primary election. Justice Hugo Black, who delivered the opinion of the Court, noted that the Supreme Court had previously invalidated an identical primary law in Texas in *Smith v. Allwright*, 321 U.S. 649 (1944).

Black noted that the white primary system had so effectively barred African Americans from voting that the "interpretation test" as a device for disenfranchisement was ignored. Due to an increase in the number of registered African American voters and the 1954 Supreme Court decision which invalidated the laws upholding school segregation, Louisiana sought new ways to bar African Americans from voting. A "Segregation Committee" was created by the Louisiana Legislature for this purpose.

In *Harman v. Forssenius*, 380 U.S. 528 (1965), the Supreme Court held that Virginia's voter registration policies were unconstitutional. Virginia eliminated the poll tax requirement for federal elections and substituted a provision in which the federal voter could qualify either by paying the customary poll tax or by filing a certificate of residence six months before the election. The Supreme Court held that these new restrictions which were implemented by Virginia were in violation of the Twenty-fourth Amendment.

The poll tax in Virginia was implemented for the purpose of preventing African Americans from being able to vote. There was no secret about this at all. At the Virginia Constitutional Convention of 1902, the sponsor of the suffrage plan in which the poll tax was included, stated very frankly: "Discrimination! Why, that is precisely what we propose; that, exactly, is what this Convention was elected for—to discriminate to the very extremity of permissible action under the limitations of the Federal Constitution, with a view to the elimination of every negro voter who can be gotten rid of, legally, without materially impairing the numerical strength of the white electorate." This statement, which was delivered by Carter Glass, is very revealing not only because it demonstrated that there was no pretense about denying African Americans the ability to vote, but also because it demonstrated that racist legislators were trying to discriminate as much as they could within the limits of the Constitution.

In *Harper v. Virginia Board of Elections*, 383 U.S. 663 (1966), the Supreme Court overturned the prior ruling in *Breedlove v. Suttles*, 302 U.S. 277 (1937) holding that poll taxes violated the Equal Protection Clause of the Fourteenth Amendment and were therefore unconstitutional. In his dissent, Justice Hugo Black wrote that the Court's decision was "to no extent based on a finding that the Virginia law as written or as applied is being used as a device or mechanism to deny Negro citizens of Virginia the right to vote on account of their color." Black explained that if "the record could support a finding that the law as written or applied has such an effect, the law would of course be unconstitutional as a violation of the Fourteenth and Fifteenth Amendments and also 42 U. S. C. § 1971 (a)." Black appeared to disagree with the Court's ruling "that the Equal Protection Clause necessarily bars all States from making payment of a state tax, any tax, a prerequisite to voting." In Black's view *Breedlove* was correctly decided because the "mere fact that a law results in treating some groups differently from others does not, of course, automatically amount to a violation of the Equal Protection Clause."

The Voting Rights Act of 1965 was passed to enforce the voting rights provisions of the Fifteenth Amendment. The second section of the Fifteenth Amendment gave Congress the power to enforce the Fifteenth Amendment through passing the appropriate legislation, although it took pressure from the civil rights movement for Congress to finally pass legislation to protect the voting rights of African Americans. Merely just being citizens should have guaranteed African Americans equal voting rights under the law, but this was not the case. The very purpose for implementing the Fifteenth Amendment was to protect the voting rights of African Americans, but even then, additional legislation was needed to protect those voting rights.

Justice Harlan's dissent in *Civil Rights Cases* helped to highlight how selective the Supreme Court has been with which rights it has chosen to enforce. Harlan stated that "the substance and spirit of the recent amendments of the Constitution have been sacrificed by a subtle and ingenious verbal criticism." Harlan also explained "that the court has departed from the familiar rule requiring, in the interpretation of constitutional provisions, that full, effect be given to the intent with which they were adopted." Harlan continued to explain: "The purpose of the first section of the act of Congress of March 1, 1875, was to prevent *race* discrimination in respect of the accommodations and facilities of inns, public conveyances, and places of public amusement."

Justice Harlan took issue with the fact that the Supreme Court's ruling in the case was contrary to the intent with which the Fourteenth Amendment was adopted. Justice Harlan explained that section 2, article IV of the Constitution gave Congress the authority to pass the Fugitive Slave Law of 1793, which established "a mode for the recovery of fugitive slaves, and prescribing a penalty against any person who should knowingly and willingly obstruct or hinder the master, his agent, or attorney, in seizing, arresting, and recovering the fugitive, or who should rescue the fugitive from him, or who should harbor or conceal the slave after notice that he was a fugitive."

Justice Harlan's reference to the Fugitive Slave clause of the Constitution is noteworthy here because it demonstrated that the Supreme Court was willing to uphold the right of slave masters to retain control over their slaves, but the Supreme Court was much less willing to enforce constitutional measures which were designed to prevent racial discrimination. Justice Harlan noted that "the Constitution recognized the master's right of property in his fugitive slave, and, as incidental thereto, the right of seizing and recovering him, regardless of any State law, or regulation, or local custom whatsoever" and that "the right of the master to have his slave, thus escaping, delivered up on claim, being guaranteed by the Constitution, the fair implication was that the national government was clothed with appropriate authority and functions to enforce it."

Justice Harlan noted that the constitutionality of the Fugitive Slave Act of 1850, much like the Fugitive Slave Law of 1973, rested "solely upon the implied power of Congress to enforce the master's rights." Harlan continues to note that these provisions "placed at the disposal of the master seeking to recover his fugitive slave, substantially the whole power of the nation." Justice Harlan's dissent rightfully pointed out that the American judicial system found no problem with enforcing constitutional provisions which protected the right of a slave master to maintain enslaved persons as property. Fugitive slave provisions were meant to ensure that individuals who no longer wished to be enslaved had no say in the matter. Such individuals were forcibly returned if they ran away. When it came to the Fourteenth Amendment, there was much less willingness on the part of the judicial system to enforce the protections which the Constitution offered to African Americans. Fugitive slave provisions benefited slave masters, even if doing so was against the desire of the enslaved. Similarly, the Supreme Court's willingness to uphold segregation benefited racist segregationists, against the desires of those who were excluded because of these segregationist policies.

The willingness to enforce the Fugitive Slave Clause in the Constitution was demonstrated in *Prigg v. Pennsylvania*, 41 U.S. (16 Pet.) 539 (1842), which was another Supreme Court case. Edward Prigg was a citizen of Maryland who was indicted in Pennsylvania for kidnapping Margaret Morgan, an African woman who was born into slavery and escaped to Pennsylvania. Under the laws of Maryland, Morgan was a slave for life to her master, Margaret Ashmore. Prigg tracked down and captured Morgan in Pennsylvania for the purpose of returning Morgan into slavery.

By the time of this case Pennsylvania had already abolished slavery. The act which outlawed slavery stated: "All persons, as well negroes and mulattoes, as others, who shall be born within this state, shall not be deemed and considered as servants for life or slaves; and all servitude for life, or slavery of children, in consequence of slavery of their mothers, in the case of all children born within this state, from and after the passing of this act as aforesaid, shall be and hereby is utterly taken away, extinguished and for ever abolished."

The Pennsylvania law which Prigg was charged with violating stated:

If any person or persons shall, from and after the passing of this act, by force and violence, take and carry away, or cause to be taken or carried away, and shall, by fraud or false pretence, seduce, or cause to be seduced, or shall attempt so to take, carry away or seduce, any negro or mulatto, from any part or parts of this commonwealth, to any other place or places whatsoever, out of this common-wealth, with a design and intention of selling and disposing of, or of causing to be sold, or of keeping and detaining, or of causing to be kept and detained, such negro or mulatto, as a slave or servant for life, or for any term whatsoever, every such person or persons, his or their aiders or abettors, shall on conviction thereof, in any court of this commonwealth having competent jurisdiction, be deemed guilty of a felony, and shall forfeit and pay, at the discretion of the court passing the sentence, a sum not less than five hundred, nor more than one thousand dollars, one-half whereof shall be paid to the person or persons who shall prosecute for the same, and the other half to this commonwealth; and moreover, shall be sentenced to undergo a servitude for any term or terms not less than seven years, nor exceeding twenty-one years, and shall be confined and kept to hard labor, fed and clothed in the manner as is directed by the penal laws of this commonwealth for persons convicted of robbery.

The Supreme Court ultimately reversed the conviction of Prigg, holding that "under and in virtue of the Constitution, the owner of a slave is clothed with entire authority, in every state in the Union, to seize and recapture his slave, whenever he can do it without any breach of the peace, or any illegal violence." The Supreme Court concluded that the act of "Pennsylvania upon which this indictment is founded, is unconstitutional and void. It purports to punish as a public offence against that state, the very act of seizing and removing a slave by his master, which the Constitution of the United States was designed to justify and uphold."

Another issue raised in Harlan's dissent in *Civil Rights Cases* is whether or not inns can legally exclude individuals. Harlan quotes Justice Coleridge, who explained: "The innkeeper is not to select his guests. He has no right to say to one, you shall come to my inn, and to another you shall not, as every one coming and conducting himself in a proper manner has a right to be received; and for this purpose innkeepers are a sort of public servants, they having in return a kind of privilege of entertaining travellers and supplying them with what they want." Based on this, Harlan concluded that the public nature of an innkeeper's employment "forbids him from discriminating against any person asking admission as a guest on account of the race or color of that person."

The ruling in *Civil Rights Cases* was indicative of the fact that although legislation had been put in place to protect African Americans from racial discrimination, the Supreme Court tended to narrowly interpret these policies. As has been previously demonstrated, the justification for doing so was that a broad interpretation of such legislation would violate the rights of private citizens, who have the right to exclude people on the basis of race. The Supreme Court in *Civil Rights Cases* interpreted the Fourteenth Amendment to apply to State acts, as opposed to the acts of private citizens.

The maintenance of segregated facilities was justified by the "separate but equal" doctrine put forward by the Supreme Court in *Plessy*. This doctrine was successfully challenged in *Brown v. Board of Education of Topeka*, 347 U.S. 483 (1954), in which the Supreme Court held that the separate but equal doctrine could not apply to public schools because "[s]eparate educational facilities are inherently unequal." The Supreme Court further held "that the plaintiffs and others similarly situated for whom the actions have been brought are, by reason of the segregation complained of, deprived of the equal protection of the laws guaranteed by the Fourteenth Amendment."

Apart from the argument to be made about the equal quality of facilities which was addressed in *Brown*, there is also the question of equality of liberty. All American citizens should have the same protections and the same rights under the law. This should mean that public facilities which are open to white people should be just as much open and available to African Americans. Unfortunately, even after the Fourteenth Amendment granted African Americans citizenship, citizenship did not mean equality under the law. In *Brown*, the Supreme Court finally decided to hold that segregation was a violation of the Constitution.

The ruling in *Brown* was a blow against segregation, but it was also a blow to black educators as well. Bobby E. Wright explained that "as a result of the 'infamous' 1954 school desegregation decision, Blacks have lost an estimated 35,000 teaching and administrative positions in the South. Former Black principals of Black schools are now janitors in integrated schools and the same thing is going to happen to Black teachers in the North."

There is also the matter of freedom of contract, which was discussed previously in the context of employment. The Supreme Court wrestled with where to draw the limit to the freedom of contract in the context of employment. The Supreme Court was in the position of trying to balance the necessity of protecting workers, while also preserving the liberties of employers. This balance becomes even more complicated when one introduces the variable of race. Not only is there a question of protecting the workers while minimally intruding upon the rights of employers, but also the question of protecting African American workers from racial discrimination, given that at one point freedom of contract also meant freedom to discriminate on the basis of race.

Freedom of contract meant that a white employer had the freedom to deny an African American solely on the basis of race. This meant the denial of things such as employment, rent, or, denial of service, to give but a few examples. This was perfectly legal under American law prior to the abolition of slavery. There were no provisions which guarded against racial discrimination in the process of contract formation and African Americans were not regarded as being citizens. African Americans were regarded as property and, as already noted, freedom of contract meant the freedom to buy and sell that property; the freedom to buy and sell Africans. Africans were the subject of contracts but did not have any legally protected rights to freely engage in contracts for their own benefit.

The Civil Rights Act of 1866, which was passed after the abolition of slavery, finally addressed the problem regarding the lack of protection for African Americans in regard to making contracts. The 1866 act not only made African people citizens under American law, but it provided freedom of contract to all citizens. Section 1981 of the 1866 Civil Rights Act provides:

> All persons within the jurisdiction of the United States shall have the same right in every State and Territory to make and enforce contracts, to sue, be parties, give evidence, and to the full and equal benefit of all laws and proceedings for the security of persons and property as is enjoyed by white citizens, and shall be subject to like punishment, pains, penalties, taxes, licenses, and exactions of every kind, and to no other.

In theory, African Americans were just as free as white citizens to make and enforce contracts, but in practice there was still no equality. This is demonstrated by Jim Crow laws, which barred African Americans from accessing the same facilities as white people. This also included housing and employment discrimination, which adversely impacted the ability of African Americans to find shelter and to earn a living. This was the very thing which the Civil Rights Act of 1866 was meant to prevent, but, as was typically the case with legislation that was meant to prevent racial discrimination, the Supreme Court applied a very narrow view regarding when such protections against racial discrimination applied.

Patterson v. McLean Credit Union, 491 U.S. 164 (1989) offers an example of the Supreme Court's very narrow approach to interpreting the protections offered by § 1981. Brenda Patterson, an African American woman, was employed by McLean Credit Union as a teller and a file coordinator. After being laid off in 1982, Patterson commenced a suit against her former employer. She alleged that Mclean Credit Union, in violation of 14 Stat. 27, 42 U.S.C. § 1981, had harassed her, failed to promote her to an intermediate accounting clerk position, and then discharged her because of her race. Patterson also claimed this conduct amounted to an intentional infliction of emotional distress, actionable under North Carolina tort law. The District Court determined that a claim for racial harassment is not actionable under § 1981 and declined to submit that part of the case to the jury.

The Supreme Court held that Patterson did not have a claim under § 1981, given that the scope of this statute prohibited the "mak[ing] and enforce[ment]" of contracts alone. Based on the language of § 1981, Justice Anthony Kennedy explained: "Where an alleged act of discrimination does not involve the impairment of one of these specific rights, § 1981 provides no relief. Section 1981 cannot be construed as a general proscription of racial discrimination in all aspects of contract relations, for it expressly prohibits discrimination only in the making and enforcement of contracts." The Supreme Court ultimately held that Patterson's claim was not actionable under § 1981 because the conduct which she alleged was not related to the formation of the contract.

Peterson alleged that she was subjected to various forms of racial harassment from her supervisor. This included being periodically stared at for several minutes at a time; being given too many tasks, which led to her complaining that she was under too much pressure; the tasks that she was given were sweeping and dusting tasks which were not given to white employees; and she also alleged that she was passed over for promotion. Justice Kennedy explained that with "the exception perhaps of her claim that respondent refused to promote her to a position as an accountant [...] none of the conduct which petitioner alleges as part of the racial harassment against her involves either a refusal to make a contract with her or the impairment of her ability to enforce her established contract rights." Justice Kennedy also explained: "Interpreting § 1981 to cover post-formation conduct unrelated to an employee's right to enforce his or her contract, such as incidents relating to the conditions of employment, is not only inconsistent with that statute's limitation to the making and enforcement of contracts, but would also undermine the detailed and well crafted procedures for conciliation and resolution of Title VII claims."

The Supreme Court's ruling in *Patterson v. McLean Credit Union* held that § 1981 does not apply to discrimination which occurs after the contract has been formed. In other words, § 1981 ensures that African Americans have the freedom to enter into employment contracts, but are not protected from being discriminated against after being employed. Based on this interpretation, § 1981 does not offer unlimited protection against racial discrimination and employers are free to discriminate, just so long as they do so after the contract has been formed, at least where § 1981 is concerned. The other statute which provides protection against employment discrimination is Title VII.

The passage of the Civil Rights Act of 1964 was a landmark moment in the civil rights movement and one of the provisions of this act was Title VII. Title VII of the Civil Rights Act of 1964 prohibits employers from discriminating against employees on the basis of race, color, religion, sex or national origin. Since the passage of the Civil Rights Act of 1964, the Supreme Court has, on more than one occasion, ruled in ways which would make it more difficult for employees to prevail under Title VII or Title VII related claims. One example of this was the ruling in *Price Waterhouse v. Hopkins*, 490 U.S. 228 (1989). Ann Hopkins brought a lawsuit against her employer, Price Waterhouse, alleging sex discrimination pursuant to Title VII. Hopkins was the only female candidate proposed for partnership in 1982 out of the eighty-eight persons proposed for partnership. She was denied the partnership and alleged that she was discriminated against on the basis of her sex.

The partners in Hopkins' office praised her character as well as her accomplishments, but Hopkins was also known for her abrasive behavior. Hopkins' poor interpersonal skills ultimately doomed her bid for partnership. Despite her professional success and strong qualities, Hopkins was described as being "sometimes overly aggressive, unduly harsh, difficult to work with, and impatient with staff."

The Supreme Court noted that there was evidence to demonstrate that some partners reacted strongly to Hopkins' behavior because she was a woman. She was described as being "macho" and another partner suggested that she "overcompensated for being a woman". Several partners criticized her use of profanity. One partner suggested that those partners objected to her swearing only "because it's a lady using foul language." Hopkins was told that if she wanted to improve her chances she had to "walk more femininely, talk more femininely, dress more femininely, wear make-up, have her hair styled, and wear jewelry."

Based on the facts of the case, Price Waterhouse did have legitimate concerns about Hopkins' interpersonal skills, which were assessed when determining whether or not to make her a partner. Yet, much of the negative response to Hopkins' behavior was based on sex stereotyping. The problem was not merely Hopkins' behavior, but that the partners believed that it was improper for a woman to behave in the manner that she was behaving. For this reason, one of the questions addressed by the Supreme Court in this case was whether or not Hopkins could still prevail on her sexual discrimination claim, despite the fact that Price Waterhouse articulated a legitimate reason for why Hopkins was denied partnership.

The Supreme Court looked at the language of Title VII, which prohibited an employer from making an adverse decision against an employee "because of such individual's . . . sex." The Supreme Court concluded that the phrase "because of" in Title VII meant "but-for causation." Justice Brennan concluded that in "determining whether a particular factor was a but-for cause of a given event, we begin by assuming that that factor was present at the time of the event, and then ask whether, even if that factor had been absent, the event nevertheless would have transpired in the same way."

This ruling meant that a defendant could escape liability if the defendant is able to prove that but for the alleged discrimination, the plaintiff would not have suffered an adverse employment action—examples of an adverse employment action include being discharged, demoted, or denied for a position. Brennan explained that "once a plaintiff in a Title VII case shows that gender played a motivating part in an employment decision, the defendant may avoid a finding of liability only by proving that it would have made the same decision even if it had not allowed gender to play such a role." In *Price Waterhouse*, the defendant merely needed to demonstrate that Hopkins would have still been denied for partnership even if her gender did not play a motivating factor. The ruling in *Price Waterhouse* allowed defendants to escape liability through proving that a legitimate reason motivated the employment decision, even if race, gender, religion, or other classes protected under Title VII were taken into consideration as well, while also imposing a higher standard for plaintiffs to meet in order to prevail in Title VII cases. Though *Price Waterhouse* was a gender discrimination case, the ruling also applied to racial discrimination cases under Title VII as well.

Congress passed the Civil Rights Act of 1991, which overturned the Supreme Court's narrow interpretation of Title VII in *Price Waterhouse*. Section 107(a) of the 1991 Civil Rights Act Amendment provides that an "unlawful employment practice is established when the complaining party demonstrates that race, color, religion, sex, or national origin was a motivating factor for any employment practice, even though other factors motivated the practice."

The 1991 civil rights bill made it easier for plaintiffs to prevail in Title VII discrimination cases by overturning the "but-for" requirement which the Supreme Court imposed in *Price Waterhouse*. The Supreme Court ruled, however, that a but-for causation analysis applied to retaliation cases, even if such cases arose out of an alleged violation of Title VII. The Supreme Court made this ruling in *University of Texas Southwestern Medical Center v. Nassar*, 570 U.S. 338 (2013).

Dr. Naiel Nassar, a physician of Middle Eastern descent who was both a University faculty member and a hospital staff physician, claimed that Dr. Levine, one of his supervisors at the University, was biased against him on account of his religion and ethnic heritage. Nassar complained to Dr. Fitz, Levine's supervisor, but after he arranged to continue working at the hospital without also being on the University's faculty, he resigned from his teaching post and sent a letter to Fitz and others, stating that he was leaving because of Dr. Levine's harassment.

Nassar filed a suit alleging Title VII violations. The first claim was a status-based discrimination claim under §2000e–2(a), claiming that Dr. Levine's racially and religiously motivated harassment resulted in his constructive discharge from the University. The second claim was that Dr. Fitz's effort to prevent the hospital from hiring him was in retaliation for complaining about Dr. Levine's harassment, in violation of §2000e–3(a).

Regarding Nassar's retaliation claim, the Supreme Court addressed the question of whether or not the lessened causation standard applied by Congress' statutory amendment to the Civil Rights Act of 1964 applied to retaliation claims. Justice Anthony Kennedy stated of the new standard imposed by Congress' 1991 act: "An employee who alleges status-based discrimination under Title VII need not show that the causal link between injury and wrong is so close that the injury would not have occurred but for the act. So-called but-for causation is not the test. It suffices instead to show that the motive to discriminate was one of the employer's motives, even if the employer also had other, lawful motives that were causative in the employer's decision." Justice Kennedy explained that prior to *Nassar*, the Supreme Court had not addressed the question of the causation showing required to establish liability for a Title VII retaliation claim. For this reason, the Supreme Court relied on its prior ruling in *Gross v. FBL Financial Services, Inc.*, 557 U.S. 167 (2009).

In *Gross*, the Supreme Court held that the Age Discrimination in Employment Act of 1967 (ADEA) required that the plaintiff prove that the plaintiff's age was the but-for cause of the prohibited conduct, much like the standard set by the Supreme Court in *Price Waterhouse*. The ADEA provides that "'[i]t shall be unlawful for an employer . . . to fail or refuse to hire or to discharge any individual or otherwise discriminate against any individual with respect to his compensation, terms, conditions, or privileges of employment, because of such individual's age.'" The Supreme Court held that the "because of" phrase in the ADEA meant that a but-for standard applied to the ADEA. Therefore, for a plaintiff to prevail in an ADEA claim, the plaintiff must demonstrate but for the plaintiff's age, the defendant would have not engaged in the adverse employment action. This also means that a defendant can escape liability by demonstrating that there was a non-discriminatory, legitimate reason for why the action was taken.

The Supreme Court noted that the ruling in *Gross* was instructive in the case of *Nassar*. Moreover, Justice Kennedy noted that "Title VII's antiretaliation provision, which is set forth in §2000e–3(a), appears in a different section from Title VII's ban on status-based discrimination." For this reason, the Supreme Court did not apply the 1991 act by Congress. Title VII's retaliation provision provides: "It shall be an unlawful employment practice for an employer to discriminate against any of his employees . . .

because he has opposed any practice made an unlawful employment practice by this subchapter, or because he has made a charge, testified, assisted, or participated in any manner in an investigation, proceeding, or hearing under this subchapter."

The Supreme Court applied a "but-for" causation standard to Title VII's retaliation provision. This meant that although employment discrimination claims which arose under Title VII no longer required a "but-for" standard, if an employer were to retaliate against an employee for complaining about discrimination, the employee would have to meet the "but-for" standard set by the Supreme Court. As explained before, the Supreme Court applies the "but-for" standard due to the language of Title VII, but this interpretation of the language of Title VII is one which frustrates the very goal which Title VII was meant to accomplish.

For African people, becoming equal citizens and enjoying the rights which are guaranteed to an American citizen under the Constitution required an extensive overhaul of America's laws, but even then struggles persisted as many of these laws were not strictly enforced and it, as has been demonstrated, the Supreme Court often interpreted these laws in such a manner as to diminish the ability of these laws to protect African Americans from the very racial discrimination which the laws were designed to prohibit. Wright referred to African Americans as a legally created people because of the fact that legislation had to be implemented in order for African Americans to become citizens, but even with this legislation in place, the legal rights of African Americans continue to be held in a very precarious balance.

American capitalism and racism operate together to not only discriminate against the African American population, but to restrict opportunities for African Americans to ensure that African Americans are at a disadvantage when compared to other workers within the system.

Anti-Capitalism and the Struggle Against Racism

After relocating to Guinea, Stokely Carmichael adopted the name Kwame Ture and became a member of the All-African People's Revolutionary Party. As an activist in the United States, Ture called for Black Power. The concept of Black Power was articulated in a book which Ture co-wrote with Charles Hamilton. After moving to Guinea, Ture adopted the ideology of Nkrumahism-Toureism which was based on the political ideologies of Kwame Nkrumah of Ghana and Sekou Toure of Guinea. One of the most important aspects of Nkrumahism-Toureism as espoused by Kwame Ture is the importance of placing the culture of African people at the center of the Pan-African liberation struggle. Nkrumahism-Toureism is a socialist ideology rooted in the historical and cultural experiences of African people. In this regard, Nkrumahism-Toureism distinguishes itself from other anti-capitalist ideologies such as Marxism, Marxism-Leninism, and Maoism.

Ture saw the tendency towards unification as being an innate evolutionary process which was interrupted by colonialism and slavery. As such, Ture argued that the unification of Africa could now only be obtained through a revolutionary process rather than an evolutionary one. Indeed, throughout Africa there was a process of nation building which produced large multiethnic kingdoms. In West Africa, several large multi-ethnic empires had emerged, such as the empires of Mali and Songhai. In South Africa, Dingizwayo was working towards uniting the disunited and warring tribes. Dingizwayo served as a mentor for Shaka who would later develop the Zulu Empire. These are just some examples to illustrate the point which Ture made. Walter Rodney explained: "All of the large states of nineteenth-century Africa were multiethnic, and their expansion was continually making anything like 'tribal' loyalty a thing of the past, by substituting in its place national and class ties."

As Ture noted, Africa's evolutionary process was interrupted by colonialism. Colonialism also imposed the system of capitalism on African societies. Whereas capitalism emerged as a product of

Europe's own historical development, Africa was brought into the global capitalist economic system via colonialism. This was accompanied by a very vicious exploitation of Africa's resources and labor.

European exploitation of African resources led to the creation of "monoculture" economies or nations which were dependent on the production of a single crop or resource. African nations often produced whatever was beneficial to the colonialists and this mode of economic production severely limited the potential of post-colonial African nations. For instance, the colonial Gold Coast produced cocoa. In the independent Ghana (formerly the Gold Coast), cocoa remained the main export, although Kwame Nkrumah worked towards diversifying Ghana's agriculture. Groundnuts accounted for as much as 90% of the revenue of Senegal and Gambia. Liberia was dependent on rubber.

In general, Africans were paid for their labor,—apart from the cases of forced slave labor, which will be discussed later—but this pay was so insignificant that the Africans were working for almost nothing. For example, in Uganda the African peasants worked for hours to cultivate cotton and they were paid so little that the price of the finished cotton shirt was more than they could even afford. One French official remarked: "I have always noticed that whenever the budget of a native family was properly and regularly kept, it never managed to make ends meet. The life of a native is, in fact, a miracle." The lack of pay that Nigerian workers received resulted in strikes such as the 1949 Enugu coal mine strike. In one of the areas where the miners were striking the police opened fire, killing 21 miners and injuring 51.

Africans were also given little compensation for whatever losses that they endured. In 1934 when 41 Africans were killed in a gold mine accident in the Gold Coast, their families were given 3 pounds each as compensation. On top of the poor pay and lack of compensation, Africans were also heavily taxed. These taxes, along with the little pay that the Africans received, allowed the Europeans to recover for the military costs of conquering Africa and maintaining their colonies. In essence, Africans were paying for their own exploitation. The Europeans would tax certain items such as cattle, houses, and in some cases the people were taxed.

There were also instances in which Africans were forced to work against their will. Africans were forced, by various methods, to work for the Europeans. One means of forcing Africans to work for the colonies was by controlling the food supply. In colonies such as Kenya and Rhodesia, the Africans were banned from growing cash-crops so that their labor was used solely for the Europeans. In French Equatorial Africa the French banned the Mandja people from hunting and they were forced to turn their attention to cultivating cotton. Colonel Grogan, a settler in Kenya, stated of the Kikuyu: "We have stolen his land. Now we must steal his limbs. Compulsory labour is the corollary of our occupation of the country." The Maasai people in Kenya also lost their land to the white settlers and they were forced to relocate to settlements. The colonial government claimed that the Maasai had agreed to surrender their land, but when the Maasai challenged this in court the court ruled against them.

Given the realities of colonialism in Africa, many of the revolutionary anti-colonial leaders in Africa developed an anti-colonial vision which was also anti-capitalist in nature. One example of this was Amilcar Cabral who fought against Portuguese colonialism in Guinea-Bissau.

Cabral addressed the pre-colonial class structure in Guinea-Bissau, which was not uniformly developed. The Balanta people developed what Cabral called "a horizontal society," which meant that there were no classes above another. There were no great chiefs until the Portuguese arrived and made chiefs for the Balanta people. Regarding the individual accumulation of wealth, Cabral stated: "Balanta society is like this: the more land you work, the richer you are, but the wealth is not to be hoarded, it is to be spent, for one individual cannot be much more than another."

Cabral explained that others had vertical societies, in which there was a chief at the top. The chiefs along with religious leaders formed what Cabral called a class. Then there were professionals such as clobbers, blacksmiths, and goldsmiths who did not have the same rights as those at the top. Cabral explained that by tradition, "anyone who was a goldsmith was even ashamed of it—all the more if he were a 'griot' (minstrel)."

Below the professionals there were those who tilled the ground. The tillers tilled the ground for the chiefs. Cabral explained that in Fula and Manjaco society, chiefs were linked to God and for this reason held authority over the tillers. Among the Majaco people, a tiller could not till without the chief's order.

Cabral noted that the nature of Fula society was structured to maintain this class hierarchy, but this is not to suggest that there were not conflicts. Cabral explained that there have been major peasant uprisings among the Fula people. In one instance, Mussa Molo overthrew a king and took the king's place. Cabral noted that this overthrow did not result in a significant structural change because Mussa Molo kept the same laws in place.

Cabral was forced to confront contradictions between ethnic groups, which were displayed not only in terms of different social structures among the various ethnic groups, but also in terms of prior military conflicts among the ethnic groups. Cabral explained that the Fula and Mandinga, unlike the Balanta, had chiefs. Cabral also explained that the majority of Fula and Mandinga in Guinea-Bissau were persons who became Mandinga and Fula. Cabral spoke of individuals being "Mandingized" as a result of Mandingo conquests.

The expansion of kingdoms resulted in wars and conquests in which certain conquered groups became absorbed into the dominant group. Wars and conflicts of this nature were an aspect of Africa's own internal development, but such conflicts were used by the Portuguese to provoke divisions among the people as part of the colonial divide and conquer tactic which kept Africans divided among each other thereby making it easier for Europeans to conquer and subjugate African people. Cabral sought to unite the society around chasing out the Portuguese colonizers.

Cabral also sought to unify the three classes in his society: the ruling class, the artisan class, and the peasant class. He recognized that this did not mean that everyone had to be united. In fact, Cabral acknowledged that there were certain self-interested individuals who "are afraid of losing their privileges in favour of the struggle."

The struggle for independence which Cabral was engaged in was a very brutal one. The Portuguese resorted to torture and massacre, including a massacre in 1959, which killed fifty

Africans. Despite this, Cabral still sought to negotiate a peaceful end to the conflict. Carlos Schwarz quoted Cabral as stating that "both sides speak Portuguese and could understand each other each quickly". Cabral also worked to win over the Portuguese soldiers against whom his people fought. In a message to the Portuguese colonial army, Cabral asserted that his people were "not the enemy of the Portuguese people." He continued to explain: "You are the sons of the Portuguese people, but you are being used by the colonialists as tools to kill our people, in order to try to prevent us being free and masters of our own land."

Cabral clarified that the struggle was a struggle against the capitalist ruling class in Portugal, which oppressed Africans in the colonies, and which oppressed the Portuguese people. Cabral explained that this ruling class "exploits the people of Portugal as much as it exploits us." Cabral also explained that the enemy which confronted Africans was not the Portuguese people or Portugal itself, but Portuguese colonialism represented by the fascist government of Portugal.

Cabral noted that Africans answered the Portuguese attempt to bring religion and civilization "with weapons in hands", so there is no mistaking the fact that Cabral was prepared to engage in a serious armed struggle against Portugal for the liberation of his people, but given his Marxist views, Cabral was clearly articulating that he was fighting against a particular class of Portuguese society and not against all Portuguese people.

Of course, we could go back even further than Cabral to point to a class-centered approach to Pan-Africanism and anti-colonialism. The Fifth Pan-African Congress represented a shift towards a more class conscious approach. This shift can be seen in W.E.B. Du Bois' own ideological growth. Du Bois, who was an organizer in the previous four congresses, had favored what he called the "Talented Tenth." He described his belief as follows in *Dusk of Dawn*: "I believed in the higher education of a Talented Tenth who through their knowledge of modem culture could guide the American Negro into a higher civilization. I knew that without this the Negro would have to accept white leadership, and that such leadership could not always be trusted to guide this group into self-realization and to its highest cultural possibilities."

Du Bois had expressed the view that "the power of this aristocracy of talent was to lie in its knowledge and character and not in its wealth." In *Souls of Black Folk*, Du Bois had expressed the view that the "worker must work for the glory of his handiwork, not simply for pay; the thinker must think for truth, not for fame." Du Bois was not someone who expressed the view that leadership should be determined by wealth or that individuals should be driven by wealth and fame, but at this particular point Du Bois also was not very conscious of class relations. In time Du Bois would critique his earlier vision of the Talented Tenth, explaining: "The problem which I did not then attack was that of leadership and authority within the group, which by implication left controls to wealth—a contingency of which I never dreamed. But now the whole economic trend of the world has changed. That mass and class must unite for the world's salvation is clear. We who have had least class differentiation in wealth, can follow in the new trend and indeed lead it."

Kwame Nkrumah served as the joint secretary to the Fifth Pan-African Congress along with George Padmore, a Trinidadian—Du Bois attended this congress as well. One of the declarations at this Congress stated: "The Fifth Pan-African Congress calls on intellectuals and professional classes of the Colonies to awaken to their responsibilities. The long, long night is over. By fighting for trade union rights, the right to form co-operatives, freedom of the press, assembly, demonstration and strike, freedom to print and read the literature which is necessary for the education of the masses, you will be using the only means by which your liberties will be won and maintained. Today there is only one road to effective action—the organization of the masses."

In *Africa Must Unite*, Kwame Nkrumah wrote that a number of political demonstrations and strikes took place throughout Africa prior to World War II. During the 1940s, many organizations were formed, such as the National Council of Nigeria and the Cameroons, as well as the Nyasaland National Congress. In the Gold Coast, Nkrumah formed the Convention People's Party. Nkrumah noted that these parties acted as unifying forces in Africa. In Nkrumah's view, the C.P.P. represented the ordinary, common folk of Ghana. He contrasted this with the opposition party which was supported by lawyers and other conservative professionals who did not understand the new mood of the people.

Nkrumah had previously served as secretary of the United Gold Coast Convention (U.G.C.C.). Nkrumah stated that the leaders of the U.G.C.C. were frightened to learn that Nkrumah had spearheaded a mass movement. He explained: "They had wanted me to build up a movement whose ranks would not question their self-assumed right to political leadership, but would nevertheless provide a solid enough base for them to pose as the national champions in pressing for constitutional change. It was when the leaders of the U.G.C.C. demanded I get rid of the mass following I had built up, that I withdrew from their secretariat, and formed the Convention People's Party."

Nkrumah was describing a conflict which would become more pronounced in the post-colonial period. During colonialism, there arose a class within the African population which managed to carve out a comfortable living for themselves as professionals within the colonial system. This was the class which seized power following the formal end of colonialism. This new neo-colonial class continues to enjoy a degree of comfort as the African masses continue to struggle.

The roots of this neo-colonial class can be traced to the development of colonialism in Africa. There were various Africans who aligned with and supported colonialism for one reason or another. Bishop Samuel Ajayi Crowther in Nigeria, for example, defended colonialism because it brought Christianity to Africa. This is an example of the fact that some Africans embraced colonialism. The nationalist leaders in Africa were generally opposed to colonialism, although many of these nationalist leaders were themselves highly influenced by colonialism. The result was that these leaders opposed colonialism, but also kept the colonial system in place once in power. These anti-colonial leaders would prove themselves to be little more than opportunists who fought colonialism so that they could replace the colonizers as exploiters of the African masses.

In Ghana, Nkrumah sought to pursue a path of socialist development to guarantee full employment, good housing, equal educational opportunity, and cultural advancement for all. Nkrumah believed that the government had to "play the role of main entrepreneur in laying the basis of the national economic and social advancement." In Nkrumah's view, to turn the country over to private interests would be an act of "betraying the trust of the great masses of our people for the greedy interests of a small coterie of individuals, probably in alliance with foreign capitalist." It was indeed foreign capitalists who overthrew Nkrumah in a coup. The United States and other Western powers would not tolerate any attempt to transform Africa through socialism, especially in the 1960s as the United States was waging its ideological struggle with the Soviet Union.

That the nationalist movements in Africa at the time embraced socialism is hardly surprising considering that many African leaders recognized that capitalism formed the economic basis of the very colonial system which they had fought. For leaders such as Nkrumah, socialism promised an alternative path of development which was different from the exploitative capitalist system. It was also the case that African leaders who opted to embrace socialism did not all share the same vision regarding what socialism in their respective nations was to look like. There were others who rejected socialism, as well.

There was a class of African leadership which were very content with continuing the colonial system, so that they also benefitted from the exploitation of their people. One example of this was Joseph Mobutu of the Congo, which he renamed to Zaire. Zaire was like Mobutu's personal property, mirroring the way Leopold II had controlled the Congo. Mobutu made a fortune from exploiting his people while also enjoying close relations with the Western world, especially with the United States and France. American military aid assisted Mobutu to stay in power in the face of numerous attempts to overthrow him. American President Ronald Reagan described Mobutu as "a voice of good sense and good will." Reagan's successor, George H.W. Bush, described Mobutu as "one of our most valued friends." Bush added, "I was honored to invite President Mobutu to be the first African head of state to come to the United States for an official visit during my presidency."

This honored guest of the White House plundered his nation's treasury to the point that by 1993 there was no money to pay the army and state officials. Soldiers responded to this by rioting. They looted shops, homes, and government buildings, killing hundreds in the process. Corruption and theft reached a point where the American embassy advised its staff not to unlock their car doors or roll down their windows when stopped by the police at roadblocks. They recommended simply showing their papers through the windows of their car to avoid being robbed. By the time that Mobutu was overthrown he was one of the richest men in the world, having an estimated $4 billion. He owned a yacht, a private jet, and homes in various European countries. Mobutu certainly was not the only African leader who enriched himself as his people struggled.

The greed of these leaders was also combined with a degree of incompetence. This is why Walter Rodney stated: "Nowhere in the world do you find a scenario of politics to compare with some African and Caribbean states. One could write a scenario that is a sheer tragedy and one could write a scenario that is a comedy, and they would both be applicable." Rodney spoke of the situation in Uganda, where someone like Idi Amin who was both a buffoon and a murderer could be the president of the country. This was the sort of situation which was seen throughout the post-colonial world to varying degrees. Political leaders could be incompetent and ineffective buffoons with an unsatiable desire for adulation, which was often taken to laughably absurd levels, yet those same leaders also often engaged in the murder and torture of their own population.

In Togo under Gnassingbé Eyadéma, citizens were made to line up to clap for him four times during the day, including when he was on his lunch break. Those who were caught not clapping for him were arrested. Civil servants were also made to wear uniforms with his image on it and to dance for him. The absurdity of this would almost be humorous if not for the tortures and killings which the Togolese people had to endure simply to appease the ego of Eyadéma. This was the type of scenario which confronted post-colonial societies. These were societies run by the likes of Gnassingbé Eyadéma and Idi Amin, and "Papa Doc" in Haiti and

Mobutu in the Congo, which Mobutu had renamed to Zaire.

Independence for these colonial societies coincided with the Cold War, which was a struggle between the United States and the Soviet Union. One of the main features of this struggle was the ideological clash between the capitalism of the United States and the socialism of the Soviet Union. As African and Caribbean countries gained independence, they were also wrestling with whether to adopt capitalism or Marxism. This same question was also confronting Africans in the United States, who were beginning to question the entire capitalistic structure of the United States and who were paying close attention to the Marxist revolutions which were being carried out in other parts of the world, particularly in Cuba and in China.

In the 1960s, Malcolm X was also coming to recognize the significance of the socialist anti-colonial struggles which were being waged around the world. Though Malcolm never labeled himself as a socialist, he understood that these socialist movements were rejecting not only capitalism, but the racial oppression which accompanied capitalism. This is why Malcolm stated: "It's impossible for a white person to believe in capitalism and not believe in racism. You can't have capitalism without racism. And if you find one and you happen to get that person into a conversation and they have a philosophy that makes you sure they don't have this racism in their outlook, usually they're socialists or their political philosophy is socialism."

Malcolm further explained: "I've had an opportunity to do a lot of it in the Middle East and Africa. While I was traveling I noticed that most of the countries that had recently emerged into independence have turned away from the so-called capitalistic system in the direction of socialism. So out of curiosity, I can't resist the temptation to do a little investigating wherever that particular philosophy happens to be in existence or an attempt is being made to bring it into existence."

It was noted before that capitalism developed along with the rise of racism among the Western imperial powers. As such, the liberation struggle of African people became not only a struggle against racial oppression, but a struggle against capitalist oppression as well. For African people, the liberation struggle had to encompass both of these realities because racism had become so deeply engrained in the culture of Western capitalist nations that even white led labor movements were racist. This was why in 1959 the black members of the American Federation of Labor and Congress of Industrial Organizations (AFL–CIO) had to form their own Negro American Labor Council (NALC) under the leadership of A. Philip Randolph. Randolph complained: "It is unfortunate that some of our liberal friends, along with some of the leaders of labor, even yet do not comprehend the nature, scope, depth, and challenge of this civil rights revolution which is surging forward in the House of Labor."

Samuel Gompers, who served as the president of the AFL, wrote a pamphlet in 1901 in which he argued against "the admission of Asiatics" to the United States. On a separate occasion, he warned about "the menace of a possible overwhelming of our people by hordes of Asiatics." The AFL was meant to be an organization which sought to unite working people regardless of their color or nationality, but Gompers barred the admission of Chinese and Japanese members. Gompers defended his position by claiming that he had no prejudice against Chinese people. He claimed to have a "profound respect for the Chinese nation." He opposed Chinese immigration because of the "ills they would bring to the country." Gompers is an example of the fact that for many labor organizers in the United States, race was a more important social category than class.

Racism was one reality of the global oppression of African people, but so too was class. In "Crisis in the Periphery: Africa and the Caribbean," Rodney addressed the issue of which class was to devise and implement the program for change. He explained that in African and Caribbean societies there were two components which had power. The first of which were the working people, whose power came from their production, although in most cases this was a potential power which was yet to be actualized. The other group with power was the group which controlled the state. This group controlled the allocation of resources and the allocation of surplus in the society. The latter group Rodney referred to as the petty (or petit) bourgeoisie—this was the class to which Rodney himself belonged to. Thomas Sankara, the former president of Burkina

Faso, had described the petty bourgeoisie as a class which "often vacillates between the cause of the popular masses and that of imperialism. In its large majority, it always ends up by taking the side of the popular masses."

In Rodney's view, the working class should be the leading social group in the struggle. In his view, the petty bourgeoisie as a class is unable to lead a country anywhere except to destruction since that class was spawned from imperialism and capitalism within colonial societies. Rodney also rejected the socialist ideologies which were espoused by leaders who belonged to the petty bourgeoisie class.

Marcus Garvey offers an interesting example to note here. Garvey was a self-proclaimed believer in capitalism. He declared: "Capitalism is necessary to the progress of the world, but there should be a limit to the individual or corporate use or control of it." Garvey did not believe that individuals should possess more than they needed. In Garvey's view, "all control, use, and investment of money should be the prerogative of the State with the concurrent authority of the people." Garvey had also criticized black capitalists that enriched themselves and gave back little in return to less privileged black people. In 1924, Garvey complained: "We have not only to fight the white capitalist, but we also have to fight the capitalistic Negro. He will sell his own people into Hell the same as anybody else." Garvey was very critical of those wealthy black men who were "money hoarders" that did little to help their race.

Garvey's speeches and writings were filled with references to class struggles and even at times appeals to working class solidarity. In a 1926 editorial, Garvey wrote: "The royal and privileged classes of idlers who used to tyrannize and oppress the humble hordes of mankind are now experiencing difficulty in holding their control over the sentiment of the people."

In 1929, Garvey entered Jamaican electoral politics and formed the Peoples' Political Party (PPP). Garvey campaigned for a seat in the Kingston and St. Andrew Corporation council, but was jailed for three months for contempt by a British judge for promising to reform the bench if he was elected. Garvey was successfully elected while he was in prison, but the seat was considered vacant. Garvey returned the next year and was unopposed in his bid for the seat. Garvey also made a bid for legislative council, but was defeated in January 1930 mostly due to the fact that by 1930 the majority of the black masses still could not vote. Garvey continued to serve on the Kingston and St. Andrew Corporation council for a number of years and was even reelected in 1931, despite being out of the country.

Theodore Vincent described Garvey as a "welfare state liberal" due to the fact that the PPP took the position that workers social security, employment, and compensation in cases of injury should all be guaranteed by the government. Even before entering into politics, Garvey had expressed concern for the working class in Jamaica. In 1921, Garvey had advocated that the working class in Jamaica should "get together and form themselves into unions and organizations and elect their members for the Legislative Council."

As was stated, Garvey was a self-described capitalist, but he was also someone who was very critical of the capitalist system for its exploitative nature. Unlike African socialists, Garvey did not advocate for a revolutionary overthrow of capitalism, but he did advocate for reforms within the capitalist structure.

In closing, the liberation struggles of African people has in large part been a struggle against the capitalist system which emerged out of Europe because of the manner in which that system has exploited African people globally.

www.ingramcontent.com/pod-product-compliance
Lightning Source LLC
Chambersburg PA
CBHW051706250726